Lee Lister is a Bid and Program Manager with more than 25 year's management and consultancy experience and 20 year's program and project management experience in projects for many household names. She also has 15 years bid management experience ranging from bids for medium companies to large international and country infrastructure bids.

On the internet she is known as **"The Bid Manager"**.

Whilst working in the Far East she became a recognized expert on preparing and evaluating large World Bank Proposals (infrastructure and business process projects within developing countries). She also consulted on setting the World Bank Bid Evaluation Criteria. This expertise was acknowledged by an invitation to be the principle speaker at an International Business Development Conference in Washington, USA.

She has also consulted at very senior and level and with government officials in several countries in Asia, Europe, America and Australia. Her experience encompasses, bid management, bid evaluation, negotiation, bid training, consultancy and program management.

She is a prolific published writer of books, ebooks and articles and can easily be found on major search engines.

FastTrack© Bid Management

First published in Great Britain in 2008. Previous incarnations were used as training materials from 1998.

© **Copyright Lee Lister 2008**
All rights reserved.

No part of this publication may be reproduced, stored in a retrieval system, or transmitted in any form or by any means, without the prior permission in writing of the publisher, nor be otherwise circulated in any form of binding or cover other than that in which it is published and without a similar condition including this condition being imposed on the subsequent purchaser. This book may not be used as a training course in any format.

ISBN 978-1-4092-3815-7

Cover Photo: people of the world © Kirsty Pargeter

Other books available include:
FastTrack© Project Management
FastTrack© Bid Management

FastTrack© Bid Management

Understand how to improve your chances of winning that proposal whilst minimizing your risk and maximizing your profit.

www.Bid-Manager.com

This book is dedicated to my daughter Kerry Lister for whom I have always strived to be my best.

FastTrack© Bid Management

CONTENTS

Legal Notice _____ **9**
FastTrack© Bid Management _____ **10**
What is Bid Management? _____ **12**
   The Invitation to Tender _____ 14
SuperBid Methodology _____ **15**
   Stage Processes _____ 16
   Decision Stage _____ 17
     Bid Sponsor _____ *18*
   Strategy Stage _____ 18
   Preparation Stage _____ 19
   Pricing Stage _____ 20
   Production Stage _____ 21
Bid Reviews _____ **22**
   Legal Reviews _____ 22
   Approach Reviews _____ 22
   Quality Reviews _____ 23
   Risk Reviews _____ 23
   Risk Matrix _____ 24
Bid Controls _____ **25**
   Risk Control _____ 25
   Cost Control _____ 25
   Solution Control _____ 25
   Design Control _____ 26
   The Bid Team _____ 27
   Bid Tool Kit _____ 29
     Compliance Matrix _____ *30*
     The Pricing Model _____ *31*
     Bid Plan _____ *31*
     Caveats _____ *32*
     War Room _____ *32*

FastTrack© Bid Management

    Red Team 33
    Design Templates 33
    Bid factory 33
Bid Strategy **34**
  Bid and Cost Strategy 35
  Go/No Go 36
  Risk Levels 36
Risk **39**
  Bid Risk 39
  Contractual Risk 41
  Financial Risks 42
  Project Risks 42
  Internal Risks 43
Where to Look for Risk **44**
    Contractual Risk 44
      Each party's responsibilities & liabilities 46
      Delays and Stoppages 46
      Delay and Stoppage Process 47
      Change Control Process 47
      Dispute Process 48
      Force Majeure 48
      Copyrights 48
      Payment Schedule 49
      Penalties 50
  Financial Risk 50
  Project Risk 51
  Internal Risks 51
Risk Measurement **52**
  Risk Matrix 52
  Risk Mitigation 53
Bid Definition **55**

FastTrack© Bid Management

- Bid Structure 56
  - Executive Summary 56
  - The Best Company – it explains why you are. 57
  - Solution 57
  - Selling Hooks 57
  - Key Selling Points 58
  - Support Documentation 58
  - Caveats 58
  - Costs 58
  - Conclusion 59
  - Other Bits and Bobs 59
- **Bid Presentation** **60**
  - Preparation 61
  - The Proposal Structure 62
  - Presentation Golden Rules 63
- **Bid Production** **64**
  - Bid Administration 64
  - War Room 65
  - Assigning Work 65
  - The Red Team 66
  - Subcontractors 66
  - Costing 66
  - The Factory 67
- **Workshops** **68**
  - Workshop 1 68
  - Workshop 2 68
  - Workshop 3 68
  - Workshop 4 69
  - Scenario 1 - Croatia 69
  - Scenario 2 – New Technology 69
  - Scenario 3 – National Bingo 70

FastTrack© Bid Management

Scenario 4 – Manchester Olympics _____ 70

Scenario 5 – Contact your MP _____ 71

Scenario 6 – Reality Game Show _____ 71

Scenario 7 – Royal Move _____ 72

Scenario 8 – Major Out Sourcing _____ 72

Answers _____ **73**

Index _____ **77**

FastTrack© Bid Management

Legal Notice

We do not believe in get rich quick schemes. We do believe that business is equal parts of inspiration, hard work and luck. Every effort has been made to accurately represent our product and it's potential.

Please remember that each individual's success depends on his or her background, dedication, desire, and motivation. As with any business endeavor, there is an inherent risk of loss of capital. **There is no guarantee that you will earn any money**.

This book will provide you with a number of suggestions you can use to better guarantee your chances for success. **We do not and cannot guarantee any level of profits.**

This product is written with the warning that any and every business venture contains risks, and any number of alternatives. We do not suggest that any one way is the right way or that our suggestions are the only way. On the contrary, we advise that before investing any money in a business venture you seek counseling and help from a qualified accountant and/or attorney or lawyer.

> You read and use this product on the strict understanding that you alone are responsible for the success or failure of your business decisions relating to any information presented by our company
> Biz Guru Ltd.

FastTrack© Bid Management

Bid Management is THE skill that takes your company from Wish To Win!

In this book you will learn how to improve your chances of winning that that proposal whilst minimizing your risk and maximizing your profit. We also provide a Bid Methodology called SuperBid which will move you from Wish to Win in a logical and organized way.

We will show you how to identify and mitigate risks found lurking in that invitation to tender documents and ensure that you produce a winning proposal that highlights your company's strengths and hides your weaknesses.

This book will provide you with the key bid management skills and several workshops and question sessions and with which to practise them with.

This book consists of the following sections:
- What is bid management?
- SuperBid methodology
- Bid strategy
- Bid risk management
- Bid definition
- Bid presentation
- Bid production

FastTrack© Bid Management

There are a number of questions scattered throughout the book notes. They should be attempted within the section that you are learning. The workshops are best left until the end of the book. In addition, there are a number of exercises at the end of the book, which are designed to help you set up your bid management environment.

This book is long and has some complex facts to understand. It is best to undertake the book a section at a time.

If you require bid management consultancy, advice or assistance in writing your bid then contact us on

www.Bid-manager.com

We also write or part write tenders for small and medium companies.

Good Luck

Ms Lee Lister
The Bid Manager

What is Bid Management?

Bid Management is a high level skill that encompasses the:

- Definition and implementation of the bid strategy.
- Minimization of risk exposure.
- Definition and architecture of the proposed solution.
- Design and presentation of the bid.
- Production of the bid.

All this is achieved whilst managing a team of disparate workers, to an impossible deadline!

Bid Managers are professionals that sit between sales and project staff. Their key role is to prepare and present a proposal to a client that.

- Meets their business and cost objectives.
- Minimizes risks and maximizes profit.
- Wins the bid.

They are usually far more risk adverse than project managers and have the profitability of the company as their main aim as opposed to winning at any cost.

Their terms of reference would be:
- Manage the bid team.
- Be the company contact for the proposer.
- Be responsible for the bid from start to win (or lose).
- Manage the strategy of the bid as agreed by the bid sponsors.
- Decide on the design of the bid and ensure that this is adhered to.
- Work with the proposed project manager in designing a business and technical solution that will meet the needs of the proposer whilst still being efficient, effective and profitable, and most importantly – workable!
- Ensure that the bid reflects the company ethos, the bid strategy, the proposed project and is signed off by all involved departments.
- Ensure that the bid is correct and error free, including terminology, grammar and spelling.
- Lead the fact finding and negotiations.

QUESTION

How does Bid Management differ from Project Management?
(Answers at the end of the book)

The Invitation to Tender

This is the formal document setting out:
- What's required and when.
- The present situation.
- Constraints & benchmarks.
- Terms & conditions of the bid.
- Indicative contract.
- Bidding instructions.
- The preferred layout of the bid.

And is the normal method of starting a bid. It is normally available via:
- Postings on the internet.
- Direct request from the client.
- Adverts in newspapers, journals and periodicals.

Other options to starting a bid are as a result of:
- A request made via the sales force.
- A request resulting from existing consulting activities.
- A direct request from the client who brings a business problem to your attention.

Informal requests should be formally documented and then agreed with the client in order to ensure that everything is understood by both sides.

SuperBid Methodology

The SuperBid Methodology is a group of procedures and techniques designed to effortlessly work together in the highly charged environment of a bid preparation.

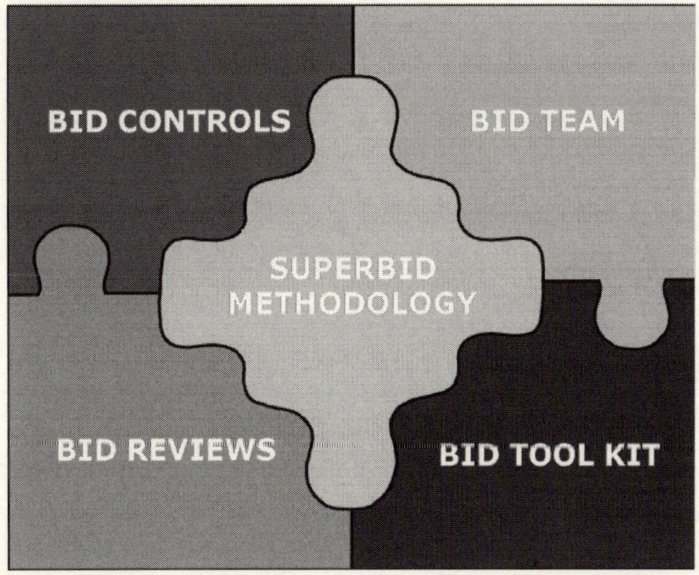

To ensure that a viable bid is produced with the minumum of risk SuperBid brings together:

– **Staged processes** – your managed movement through the bid.

– **Bid reviews** – regular checks on the bid.

– **Bid controls** – making sure all goes well.

– **An optimum bid team** – the best people to ensure the success of the bid.

– **Bid tool kit** – your tools to manage the bid.

FastTrack© Bid Management

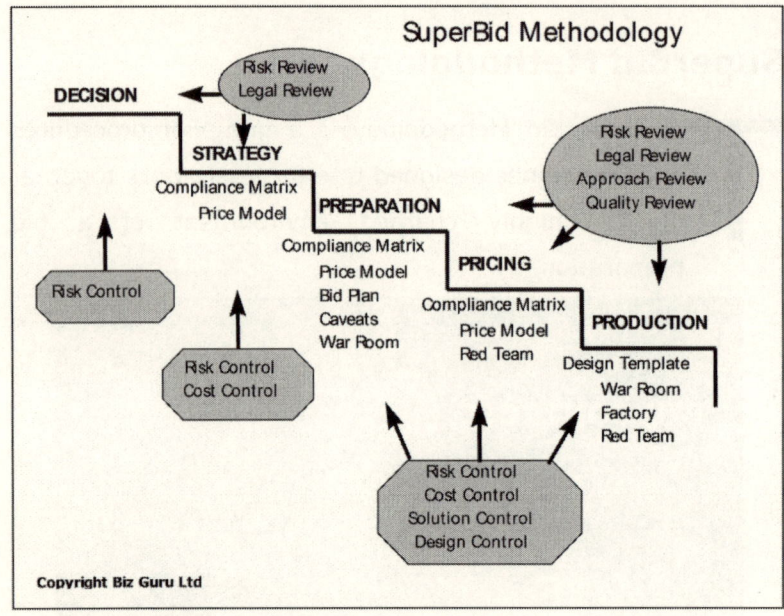

Stage Processes

SuperBid uses these stages, each with its own set of processes and products, in order to manage the bid in a modular and controlled manner:

- Decision
- Strategy
- Preparation
- Pricing
- Production

They are followed logically from one to another. In small bids two stages can be undertaken at the same time. For large bids they should be separated. In all cases the Decision and Strategy bids should be undertaken separately and be signed off before starting on the next stage.

16

Decision Stage

This stage starts when one or more of the following is received:

- The invitation to tender (ITT)
- A lead from the sales department
- Direct request from your client
- Direct request to join a bidding consortium

This stage starts when a possible bidding situation has been identified. This may be as a result of sales force activities or receiving a formal Invitation to Tender (ITT) or a Request for Information (RFI).

During this stage:

- Information of the potential and ramifications of undertaking the proposal and resulting project is gathered
- Formal meetings are held to discuss the above
- A formal Go/No Go decision is made

At this point, a Proposal Sponsor should be chosen who has authority to commit finances and resources to the bid.

The ITT should be read thoroughly and a top-level risk matrix produced. It is common to also obtain a legal opinion as well as appointing a potential project manager, whose advice is also sought.

After a review of risk, costs and potential profits a formal Go/No Go decision is taken by the Bid Sponsor and other involved managers.

Bid Sponsor
The Bid Sponsor is the senior manager of the company who has the authority to:
- Provide a bid budget.
- Provide bid staff.
- Authorize the bid proposal start and finish.
- Be the final decision in matters appertaining to the bid.
- Ensure that staff are available to undertake the bid project if won.
- Make things happen!

As can be seen from the above the Bid Sponsor is a very important person to have on board. They should be a senior manager with some gravitas and authority as well as a direct interest in winning the bid.

Strategy Stage

During this stage:
- Information of other possible bidders is gathered.
- Different ways of bidding are investigated.
- Preliminary legal reviews of the ITT are made.
- The potential bid team is discussed.
- A formal bid strategy is agreed.

FastTrack© Bid Management

Having passed a legal and risk review, and the decision to proceed (Go) been taken, the bid moves into the Strategy Stage.

The first task is to set up a strategy team that consists of the Bid Sponsor, Bid Manager and representatives from the project team and service providers as well as legal consult. This team will formalize the **Bid Strategy** - e.g. bid low versus full specification, as well as the level of compliance that fits this strategy.

These tasks are assisted by the production of the **Compliance Matrix** and **Pricing Model** in preliminary format.

In addition the proposed technical, business, project management and support solutions are formalized, having regard to the level of risk and associated cost differences. **Key Selling Points** are identified as well as **Risk Strategies.**

Preparation Stage

During this stage:
- The **bid team** and red team are set up
- The **War Room** is set up
- The **bid plan** is started
- Key documents and information are acquired
- The **design template** is agreed

FastTrack© Bid Management

During the Preparation Stage, the bid team and **red team** are agreed. The bid team is assigned work, using the Bid Plan and the preparation for the proposal begins in earnest. This stage uses several bid tools:
- Compliance Matrix
- Caveats
- Bid Plan
- Risk Matrix

All of which are discussed and explained later on in the book.

Pricing Stage

Sometimes this is the win or lose activity and great care should be taken with this stage. The primary activities are:
- Produce the pricing model – most companies use a spreadsheet based program.
- Collate costs.
- Uplift for risk – decide how much each increment of risk will increase the cost.
- Adjust for profit – use your standard profit levels and do not forget to include costs or managing your sub contractors.
- Adjust to win – do not price yourself out of the market.
- Pricing should reflect your bidding strategy.

FastTrack© Bid Management

Production Stage

Once the bid has been prepared, it needs to be produced. This is usually the longest stage in bid management and consists of:

- Collation of information is led by the **bid administrator**.
- Quality checking by the red team.
- Duplicating within the factory.
- Binding within the factory.
- Sending the bid to the client.

There are three main activities during this stage:

- **Factory** - the actual production of the original and copies of the proposal - not to be underestimated as to the time it can take.
- **Quality Review** - the final quality review for completeness, presentation and content.
- **Go/No Go** - the final decision as whether to send in the proposal.

The proposal documentation - a combination of standard documentation and the documented solutions are collated and chased for by the Bid Administrator.

Bid Reviews

To compliment these controls a number of reviews are also undertaken:

- Legal review
- Approach (price v risk v solution) review
- Quality review
- Risk review

Legal Reviews

In a bid that will cost a lot of money to produce, that relies upon an understanding of a complex RFP and sample contract, it is important to obtain a formal legal review of the terminology. Similarly the caveats you produce and any other risk mitigation actions, which have a legal impact, should be reviewed on a regular basis. It is important to remember that any formal reply to a bid as well as any discussions undertaken should be treated as a legally binding contract.

Approach Reviews

During a bid, it is important to ensure that the balance of the price, solution and level of risk always remain at a comfortable level and aligned with the bid strategy.

At the beginning of the preparation stage, before the start of the production stage an Approach review should be undertaken. Additionally whenever one or more of price, solution and level of risk changes, another Approach Review should be undertaken.

Quality Reviews

It stands to reason that you want the proposal to reflect the quality of your proposed solution, as well as your company standards. Quality reviews, held on a regular basis, would ensure that this happens.

Risk Reviews

A risk matrix is produced at the beginning of the bid process, from preliminary reading of the RFP. It is then updated to reflect the project strategy and solution chosen, as well as further detailed readings of the RFP.

Regular reviews of the risks being run, coupled with the risk mitigation actions taken, form the basis of the regular reviews.

Risk Matrix

A risk matrix is a common tool used by the project manager, although a bid manager will use a slightly different version. Use scores of 1-5, with five being higher to reflect the levels of risk as well as the likelihood of each risk.

Risk	Impact of Risk	Likelihood of Risk	Cost of *Risk	Actions
Risk 1	3	4	300k	Don't accept
Risk 2	2	1	4k	Mitigate
Risk 3	3	4	2.5k	Accept

*Cost of accepting risk, mitigating risk or how much do you have to increase your bid in order to accept the risk.

QUESTION

What is the importance of the bid reviews?

Bid Controls

To ensure a viable proposal a number of control procedures are available to you in order to ensure that your bid progresses as it should. These controls are:
– Risk control
– Cost control
– Solution control
– Design control

Risk Control

Risk controls managing your exposure to risk and are so important to a successful bid that a complete section has been assigned to this topic.

Cost Control

The preparation of a proposal within a tight time frame calls for many changes and updates. Many of these will have an impact on the costs and thus your profit level. It is vital that the Price model is regularly updated to reflect these changes and give an accurate picture.

Solution Control

Having decided upon the solution you wish to propose, it is important to ensure that this proposed solution is what is defined within the bid.

FastTrack© Bid Management

When you have a large complex bid, written by a number of different people and/or companies, then this becomes very difficult. A detailed understanding of the solution, combined with regular updates is a very important part of the bid manager's role.

To do this it is important that all participants understand their role in providing the complete solution and that their output is checked against that which is required of them.

Design Control

In order to ensure that your proposal has a uniformed corporate look, it is important that design templates are set up and circulated to all. The templates should set out, fonts, styles, paper sizes, color of paper, brands etc. Regular reviews, usually by the Bid Administrator, are made, to ensure that these templates are adhered to.

Design control also makes the collation of each member of the team's output into a final bid, that much easier as well.

FastTrack© Bid Management

> **Bid Strategy** = acceptable risk level + cost strategy + Key Selling Points + Selling Hooks + what level of non-compliance are you comfortable with?

I have purposely put this on a page of its own because it is so important!

38

FastTrack© Bid Management

The groups in the Bid Team are as follows:

– **Bid Sponsor:** As described above, this is the person within the team with the power to make things happen and sign off any bid or proposal. Sometimes, in a large or strategic bid, the Bid Sponsor will also have a group of senior managers who will advise them.

– **Bid Manager:** As mentioned above, this is the person who will drive, control and manage the bid.

– **Quality:** This person, or group, will be independent of the bid management team and responsible for the quality of the bid. They will review the quality at the end of each stage.

– **Red Team:** This team will check the whole bid to ensure that it meets quality standards and adheres to all strategic and design decisions taken. More details are given later in the book.

– **Legal:** This group give legal opinion and advice on your RFP, bid and caveats that you use.

– **Risk Management:** Larger bids have someone tasked with managing risk within the bid.

– **Bid Administration:** This person/group are charged with ensuring that each member of the team has their assigned work, sending out the designs and then collating the bid together. Greater detail of this important role is given later in the book.

– **Financial:** In many bids it is important to have a financial accountant on hand to offer advice.

– **Pricing Team:** This group are responsible for collection financial information together and setting up and updating the costing model.

FastTrack© Bid Management

- **Project Solution:** This group look at the project and how it will be managed.
- **Technical Solution:** These members provide any technical solution that is required such as a hardware structure.
- **Support and Maintenance:** If support and maintenance is also required, these people are responsible for this part of the bid.
- **Facilities:** Similarly facilities services information are provided by this group.
- **Subcontractors:** Many large bids have a number of subcontractors that also contribute to the bid. More is described about this management later in the book.

Bid Tool Kit

To make the bid process as painless as possible the SuperBid Methodology has defined a number of bid tools. These are:

- Compliance Matrix - measurement of what is asked for against what is offered.
- Pricing model - how you price the proposal.
- Bid plan - the grand plan of who does what, when.
- Caveats – how you control your risk.
- War Room - the secure area where it all happens.
- Red team - the principle review team.
- Design templates - the presentation standard and common documents.
- Bid factory - the production area.

FastTrack© Bid Management

Compliance Matrix

The key management tool used during all stages is the Compliance Matrix - a matrix table of all the required items in the ITT. This document has three main functions:

– As a control mechanism for the bid manager to ensure that all required items are included within the proposal.

– As a summary of the proposal to be used as part of the risk review, cost proposal and Go/No Go decisions.

– To highlight the Key Selling Points to the evaluator as well as include caveats and bonus items to ensure that the proposal stands out.

An example is shown below, although the actual Compliance Matrix will be much more detailed and run to several pages.

Required Item	Page Ref	Comply Yes/No	Comments
Network configuration	44 Para 5	Yes	Will comply and add extra capacity to meet future needs
Software training	48 Para 2	Yes	Software training on all packages will be provided at our offices
Hardware configuration	98 Para 3	No	The configuration requested in the ITT will not allow for future expansion. OUR COMPANY proposes our new super machines.

The Pricing Model

A Pricing Model is produced which takes into account any NPV calculations that are requested. Care should be taken to ensure that the correct level of detail is provided. The Risk Review undertaken after the production of the technical, services, business and project solutions are agreed, will produce risk costs that should also be built in.

You should be careful that you split out taxes (VAT or as appropriate to your country) and handle delivery charges as specified in the ITT. Sometimes bids can be provide on a "time and material basis" – in which case you need to place a floor and ceiling on your costs and specify exactly what time and the materials are.

Teasers - other services that can be supplied for an extra cost can also be included - although care should be taken to stipulate that these are extras!

Bid Plan

The Bid Plan is a major bid management planning and control tool used during bid preparation. With highly structured Invitations to Tender/Bid, the evaluator provides the structure of the proposal and this should be followed. In other cases you can provide your own bid structure.

The Bid Plan should be produced from the table of contents (Toc) of the proposal. Against each of the elements of this Toc should be placed the name of the contributor and the contribution deadline. This will allow the Bid Manager and Bid Administrator to keep track of contributions.

FastTrack© Bid Management

Caveats

Caveats, assumptions and exclusions are a formal, but polite way of clearly defining what risks, responsibilities and actions that you are prepared to take.

A caveat says we will do this subject to……. An assumption states what assumptions you have made in absence of clarity. An exclusion removes the activity from the proposal.

These should be ascertained, agreed and included within the proposal and controlled by the Compliance Matrix. Remember polite, succinct and legally watertight.

QUESTION

Your hardware kit does not meet all the requirements but exceeds others. How would you manage this within your Compliance Matrix?

War Room

The War Room should also be set up. This will be where your team meet and work during the fraught period ahead. It should be secure, comfortable and well equipped (well you can dream!). Computers, printers, stationery, food, drink, meeting facilities and masses of paper for charts and plans to be stuck on the wall (don't forget the blue tack!). In many bids, the War Room should also be secure.

FastTrack© Bid Management

Red Team
The Red Team are the group of people that come in at key stages and review the proposal so far. These people should not be in the bid team. It is a good idea to include the proposed project manager within this group. The Red Team should look at quality, risk exposure, project approach and general structure and make appropriate and pertinent suggestions. They should be reviewing the proposal in two ways:

- As if they had won it and had to implement the proposed project.
- From the point of view of the potential client, as how it meets their needs and how "attractive" it is to them.

Design Templates
In order to ensure that you are your proposal has a uniformed corporate look it is important that design templates are set up and circulated to all. The templates should set out, fonts, styles, paper sizes, color of paper, brands etc. In large bids, advice as to how long the various contributions should be, need also to be included. Regular reviews, usually by the Bid Administrator, to ensure that these templates are adhered to, are very important.

Bid factory
This is the room where everything is printed off, collected together, collated and duplicated. It is full of machines and people and very frenzied at the end. Set it up on a conveyor belt principle and ensure that your Bid Administer manages the mayhem and you should survive!

Bid Strategy

At senior level the Bid Strategy is put together. This strategy is at the core of what your bid will look like and what it will include. Factors to decide upon will include:

– Should we do it?

– Can we do it?

– Go/No Go.

– Cost v profit v risk decisions – do we get enough profit back to cover our costs of the bid and the risk we will take?

– Key selling points.

– Selling hooks.

– Non compliance issues.

Should we do it?
What happens if we do not do it?

– Will we lose face?

– Lose the option to bid on further bids?

– Upset the client?

– Show our weaknesses?

– Show our strengths for little return?

– Take too much risk?

QUESTION

Can you think of a situation when your company will go ahead with a bid that will lose money?

FastTrack© Bid Management

Can we do it?

Are the client requirements?

– Feasible – that is can they be done?

– Technically possible?

– Worth the effort? The cost of bidding means that you cannot chase every ITT?

– Fit into your company profile? Your company has a recognizable brand and a group of products. To move out of this arena takes considerable thought and probably some great cost? Although sometimes companies want to move away from their core business e.g. the move from hardware selling towards system integration.

– Appropriate for your client? Sometimes clients are their own worst enemies. No one will thank you for selling something that will not work and is not really what they want.

Bid and Cost Strategy

Your strategy is a combination of:

– Bid high and provide them with a high quality and complete solution.

– Bid low with minimum compliance and thus maybe win on price alone.

– Level of compliance. What do you think is the optimum mix of products and services that will meet the majority of the client's requirements and still win you the bid?

– Extras. What other extras can you offer your potential client – maybe something that your competitors cannot?

35

FastTrack© Bid Management

What to leave out? Sometimes when trying to get to an optimum bid price, some of your offerings need to be stripped out and maybe offered as extras.

Go/No Go

Remember there are many cases where a bid should not go ahead, particularly if it is going to be costly to produce.
Factors to consider about whether to bid
- Possible profit Vs risks.
- What are the chances of success?
- Political or sales needs to bid.
- What happens if you do not bid?
- Other benefits of bidding.

Risk Levels

- What level of risk is acceptable?
- What kinds of risks are acceptable?
- How do we cost the risks we accept?

These all differ for each company. Your bid sponsor will be the final guide.

Key Selling Points
What should we emphasize?
- What is your company best at?
- How will your bid beat your competitors?
- Do you have a unique advantage?
- What do you think is the client's key requirement?
- Do you have a tempter to increase your total take on the bid?

36

FastTrack© Bid Management

Selling Hooks

What can we offer in order to attract extra spend? Look at the client's real needs and wants as well as what your rivals are better at. In particular look at the:
- Objectives of the ITT.
- Market forces and constraints.
- Budget.
- Future needs of the client.

Can you place in the bid, some nice goodies that the client will need/want in the future, that you can offer now? This is not something like a holiday in Bermuda! Think upgrades, better kit, free consultancy, help after implementation, train-the-trainer books etc. Your aim is to increase the spend from your client above your reasonable bid price and maybe increase the attractiveness of your proposal.

Non Compliance

How to deal with requirements you cannot comply with
- Turn the positive into a negative.
- Explain why you cannot comply.
- Offer something else that is the same or better.
- Ignore it – not always the best option.

A short note on compliance - there are always situations where to comply with an item would be more expensive than not to comply. It is very unlikely that your bid will be 100% compliant – the skill is to work out what % compliance Vs cost of compliance – you should aim for. Sometimes to comply would be silly – clients are known to include whole shopping lists in their RFP's!

FastTrack© Bid Management

> **Bid Strategy** = acceptable risk level + cost strategy + Key Selling Points + Selling Hooks + what level of non-compliance are you comfortable with?

I have purposely put this on a page of its own because it is so important!

Risk

This section discusses the need to manage risk. The effective recognition and mitigation of risk is so important to bid management that we have taken a whole chapter to describe where you can find risk. This chapter can seem daunting at first, but you should continually refer back to it, until you can manage risk without the need to do this.

A risk is an event that is likely to cause an adverse impact to one or more of the following, if you win the bid:
- Project budget – what it is going to cost you to implement the winning solution.
- Project timeline – how long it will REALLY take.
- Project deliverables – what you have contracted to produce.
- Project resources – what you will need to get to full implementation.

Bid Risk

Managing bid risk consists of three activities:
- Identifying the risk.
- Measuring the risk.
- Mitigating the risk.

So now we have to find where the risks are, work out how large the risks are, what problems and costs they can cause and lastly, how we mitigate these risks.

FastTrack© Bid Management

Read the proposal – Now go back and read it again!!

Within the first few days of the bid life cycle –the bid manager MUST be totally familiar with the bid. Mistakes cost money, delays, and possibly winning the bid.

As you read the RFP
- Build up your matrix of compliance.
- Itemize all the requested features that may be a problem for you to provide or may present a risk to the success of the bid or the project.
- Add to the risk matrix.
- Understand how each risk may impact upon your proposed solution and your bid strategy.

Risk Strategy
You should define your risk strategy that will consist of:
- How much risk you will accept to win the bid.
- What cost you associate with each increment of risk you assume.
- What amount of risk you have managed to pass down to you sub contractors.
- How much uplift for risk, your pricing model can accept.

FastTrack© Bid Management

Risks fall into the following categories:
- Contractual.
- Financial.
- Project.
- Internal.

We will discuss these in greater detail in the following sections of this book.

Contractual Risk

Investigate the:
- Responsibilities of each party. Are they clearly identified and set out – grey areas can cost?
- Liabilities if anything goes wrong. Are you compensated for your client's mistakes and not unfairly penalized for yours?
- Delays or changes by client, self, disputes. Again they should be fair and equitable.
- Any incorrect or incomplete specification. Sometimes the RFP is not correct or even worse impossible – if you agree to them in your bid – you are contractually committed to do the impossible!
- Copyrights. Existing, new, transfer of – protect your copyrights and others!
- Force Majeure handling. This is the unexpected happening – and of course, it usually does, make sure you are not penalized.

Financial Risks

Make sure that you investigate the:

– **Payment model:** When and under what conditions you are paid. Do they pay on results, in stages, by time and materials etc.? Some payment methods are rear loaded, which means that you may be paying out for staff and kit for some time before you receive any payment.

– **Penalties:** LD's (late damages) usually for late or incorrect delivery are frequently shown in the contract. You should ensure that they are fair and that delays caused by the client do not result in penalties.

– **Pricing levels:** Ensure that you set up your pricing models to reflect when you will be delivering as well as your profit and risk etc.

– **Correct mark up on subcontractor costs**: Make sure that you mark up your sub contractor's costs to cover managing them and the risk of them not being able to do as they are required. It is usual to penalize and sue the major bidder not the sub contractor.

Project Risks

Ensure that you have identified processes to manage:

– Changes in specification such as an effective change control process.

– Client authority and representations – you need an identified client representative who is the person who will be responsible for the client's part in the project.

– Respective responsibilities – who is responsible for what? Make sure that the split between the client's responsibilities and yours are clearly defined and understood by both sides.

– Solution – is it technically feasible and supportable?

– Project approach – is it feasible and economic as well as profitable?

Internal Risks

These are the risks internal to your own company and the risks most often forgotten by inexperienced bid managers. You should identify and manage:

– **Staffing** - available skills, costs, retaining – you have got/can get enough staff can't you? It is amazing how many project managers are handed a newly won bid and then realize that they do not have the necessary skilled staff to undertake it.

– **Resources** - available, cost effective – ditto resources – remember desks, computer time etc. Once again – if you are bringing in 30 extra staff – do you have the space, desks and computers to support them?

– **Requirements** - all gathered and interpreted correctly. This is the time to read the RFP once again and ensure that you have fully understood all the client's requirements.

– **Payments schedule** - does it allow adequate cash flow? Are you being paid when you need to be paid? Are you going to have to pay tax before you receive the money? Have you taken care of currency fluctuations? Lastly, does the schedule incentivize your company?

Where to Look for Risk

Now we have looked at the types of risk there are – it is important to understand where the risks are hiding. You should look at the following areas:

– **Contractual**: This is found chiefly in the contract but also in what is written within the RFP as well as its structure. You should treat the RFP as a contract.

– **Financial:** Your pricing model or the model imposed upon you.

– **Project:** You design the project approach to meet the RFP, so to a large extent you are responsible for bringing in these risks yourself. You should pay great attention to available technology and resources.

– **Internal:** Your business processes and how you have managed the bid and intend to manage the resulting project. For example: does the bid have full buy-in at the appropriate levels and will the proposed project work?

Contractual Risk

A contract is divided into the following:

– Definitions which are how each named item is defined and usually found at the front of the contract. It is very important to read them and query the strange ones. Not everyone's idea of something is the same.

– Each party's responsibilities & liabilities.

– Change control process.

– Delay and stoppage process.

– Payment schedule & conditions.

– Dispute process.

FastTrack© Bid Management

- Force Majeure.
- Penalties.
- Copyrights.

Contractual Risk in the RFP

To identify these risks you should look specifically at these items:

- **Clearly defined requirements:** Wishy washy, poorly defined requirements often mean that there will be costly delays during the project as your client tries to match what you are producing with what they thought that they wanted.
- **Subcontractors**: Should be contracted to your companies, answerable to you and their payment schedule reflect not only their deliverables, but also your own payment schedule.
- **Changes**: It is vitally important that changes are controlled and costed for. The chief cause of project failure is the inability to manage and control costs. If a change control method is not in the contract, or worse still not mentioned. You MUST put your own change control system into your proposal, along with a fair method of being paid for changes made, as well as not being penalized for any resulting delays.
- **Price:** As you become more experienced in bid management as well as understand your clients better, you get a better idea of what price you can charge for your proposed solution. Some clients (particularly governments) pick the cheapest option. You need to ensure that any costing options you are given, covers both your profit and any risk you undertake.

- **Feasible Solution:** Are you being asked to do the impossible? Sometimes clients get a little enthusiastic or just don't understand the technology. If you are asked to do the impossible and foolishly agree then your profit, reputation and health are going to suffer.
- **Shopping Lists:** Beware of shopping lists! Some clients use the excuse to ask for everything, sometimes just to see what they can get, often because this is their only chance to spend that budget!

Each party's responsibilities & liabilities

A contract should be looked upon as a see-saw. Evenly balanced and fair to both sides. So you should investigate the following:
- Is it evenly balanced?
- Is it appropriate?
- Are you expected to be responsible/liable for matters over which you have no control?
- Does it fit with your approach?
- Can the risks be reasonably be mitigated or costed for?
- Can you pass some down to your subcontractors?

Delays and Stoppages

Delays and stoppages, of which there will always be some, cost money so:
- The terms should be fair and equitable.
- Should not be a back door out of the contract so that you are left with a partly finished project and no hope of making a profit.

FastTrack© Bid Management

Delay and Stoppage Process

What happens if there is a delay or stoppage to the project and it is not your fault? Is there:

– Financial recompense to ensure that you are not out of pocket?

– Time allowed so that you can continue the project without penalties. You should ensure that there is time allowed for you to obtain your skilled staff once again after any delay?

– Removal of penalties so that you are not penalized for matters that you have no control over?

– A change control procedure to manage these delays and stoppages?

Change Control Process

Change control manages the changes that either come from the supplier or are caused by the need to keep the project on track. Change control and delay clauses within the ITT or contract should:

– Exist – and be very clearly defined – if not define them in your bid.

– Be fair to both sides – after all you might need to make changes as well.

– Be effective so that you have a chance to review budgets and scope for any material changes.

FastTrack© Bid Management

Dispute Process

Even in the best projects, disputes can happen. There are usually several settlement levels:
- Project board.
- Project representative.
- Legal representative.
- Independent authority.

Force Majeure

Force Majeure is something that could go wrong through no fault of either of you. This would include fire, flood, rail disputes etc. Not strikes in either company though! Even in the best-run projects, things can go amiss:
- Can you anticipate what could go wrong?
- What happens during the process of "making good"?
- Who pays for the changes?
- Is there insurance for many of the potential problems?

Copyrights

Copyrights are the ownership of a newly created item, such as book, software or product. They are very important because ownership of a copyright means that no one else can legally copy you without payment to you.
- Do not give yours away.
- Do not give other people's away.
- Define what will happen to new items.
- Do not make assumptions that you will keep or own any copyright.

FastTrack© Bid Management

QUESTION

What is the difference between a copyright and an IPR (intellectual property right)?

Payment Schedule

The very important when and how much you will be paid:

– Ensure that it aids your cash flow so that you are not paying for items and not receiving payment some considerable time later.

– Pays for upfront costs. If you have major initial costs, and you probably will have, you need your payment schedule to reflect this.

– Matched to sub contractor payments. You will need to pay your sub contractors and your payment schedule needs to ensure that you make these payments out of money received!

– Is the payment flow fair and efficient and reflect the effort you are putting into the project.

– Are the conditions of payment fair and reflect the deliverables you make?

– Will they be paid promptly and is there a method of collecting payments past due?

– Will payments match transfer of ownership?

– Will you need to borrow money to undertake the project whilst awaiting payment? If you do, then you need to ensure that loan payments are included in your pricing model.

– Are you being paid in a currency that is not your own. You should undertake currency arbitrage and if it is a weak currency also take this into account in your pricing model.

49

A short note on payment schedules: You will have a lot of upfront costs if you win the bid, not least to pay for the cost of bidding. These will include resource, people to get on board, and payments for materials. Similarly, your sub contractors will want to be paid as well. Your client however will probably subscribe to the school of thought that you will work better if you only get paid at the end. The usual compromise is for a percentage to be paid on signing of the contract, with a further percentage paid on each major deliverable and the rest at the end. You need to also map out your possible cost schedule and make sure that these match the payment schedule.

Penalties
Penalties – often called LD's, are usually enforced for late delivery or poor quality deliverables.
- Is the process fair?
- Are the penalties appropriate?
- Are all the conditions spelt out?
- Are there similar penalties on the client?

Penalties have a way of quickly building up and are a source of disputes with the client. Ensure that they are fair before you start.

Financial Risk
It is very important that your pricing model is set up correctly. Does your pricing model include:
- Overheads.
- Project & sub contractor risk.

- Reasonable profit.
- Possible delays & losses.
- Tax implications.
- Currency hedging.
- Cash flow and NPV allowances.

Project Risk

Check you project approach for

- **Technology:** Is it appropriate and feasible – will it work and provide the solution that your client is looking for?
- **Resources:** Do you have enough? Will they be available? Are they suitable?
- **Logistics:** Look at your end-to-end delivery – can you deliver the goods on time and to budget?
- **Costs:** Have you costed for all eventualities? Will you make a profit?

Internal Risks

You don't want to be the reason that you fail do you? Do your business processes:

- Support what you are proposing?
- Ensure that people and resources will be available?
- Enable the project inception to be quick?
- Ensure that the project will run smoothly?

Risk Measurement

You have now identified your risks and, of course, written them all down in your Risk Matrix – so now we need to measure it.

Risk Matrix

A Risk Matrix is a common tool to the project manager a bid manager will use a slightly different version. A typical Risk Matrix is shown below:

As you work through your risks, note them down in column 1. Use scores of 1-5, with 5 being higher to measure the impact and likelihood of the risk. The estimated cost of each risk should then be estimated and the action needed to mitigate it included in the Risk Matrix.

Risk	Impact of Risk	Likelihood of Risk	*Risk Cost	Actions
Risk 1	3	4	300k	Don't accept
Risk 2	2	1	4k	Mitigate by xxxx
Risk 3	3	4	2.5k	Accept

*Cost of accepting risk, mitigating risk or how much do you have to increase your bid in order to accept the risk.

Risk Mitigation

There are a number of ways that you can mitigate risk. These include:

- **Cost for it** - uplift costs to take the risk into account.
- **Remove it** - qualify your reply using caveats so that you do not accept the risk.
- **Limit it** - accept only up to a limit – be it time and/or cost.
- **Work around it**- offer other solutions so as to avoid this risk.
- **Accept it**- as your responsibility and ensure that you mitigate it as much as possible.
- **Pass it on** – define it as a subcontractor risk and pass it onto your subcontractors.
- **Ignore it** – sometimes for commercial reasons, you choose to ignore the risk.

In your proposal you can treat the risks by:

- Using caveats use them to limit or cap your risk, or to make the risk more reasonable.
- Do not do it, but say why.
- Ignore it – in which case you are accepting it.
- Suggesting something else that is less risky and so less costly to the client.

In your proposed project you can mitigate risks by:

- Building in safeguards and make sure you do not follow the risky route.
- Change your approach and thus avoid it.
- Buy in expertise who can mitigate or remove the risk for you.

With your sub contractors you can:

- **Pass the risk down** – be reasonable though, you do not want to bankrupt your suppliers or sub contractors.
- **Pass the penalties down**, if they reasonably belong there.
- **Define their responsibilities**, but make them fair and clear.
- **Define their deliverables** and attach them to their payment schedule.
- **Set acceptance criteria** on their deliverables. Define the circumstances and the quality of their deliverables so that they do not get paid before producing an acceptable product.

VIP

Manage your risk and you manage your proposed solution.

Cost your risk properly and you will make a profit.

Ignore risk at your own cost!

FastTrack© Bid Management

Bid Definition

This section explains how to set up your bid and decide what you should put into the proposal.

What do we need to do?
- **Win:** by designing an outstanding bid.
- **Achieve:** by defining the optimum solution.
- **Benefit:** by pricing to make a profit.
- **Control:** the standards and progress of your bid and mitigate all risks.
- **Improve:** Strategize to seize all opportunities.

How Do We Do It?
- **Follow the structure of the RFP**. Do what you are told to do in the RFP!
- **Refer to the matrix of compliance.** This is your control tool to ensure your bid reflects what is wanted and what you can do.
- **Use the bid plan to obtain your contributions**. Manage the contributions to the bid and ensure that arrive on time.
- **Use a pricing model for the costs.** Manage your costs so you have a fair chance of winning and making a profit.
- **Refer to the bid strategy**. This is the remit from your bid sponsor.
- **Measure against risk matrix**. Manage your risks and you manage your profits.

FastTrack© Bid Management

- **Include the caveats.** Clarify just what you will do, how and what risks you will accept.
- **Include key selling points.** Show your bid off to its best.
- **Include selling hooks.** Aim to make your bid more attractive and stay with the client company for other work.

> **This is the essence of bid management - do the above and you are a bid manager.**

Bid Structure

What do we put in the proposal?
- Executive summary.
- Why your company is the best one to do it.
- How you propose to do it?
- Your selling hooks – what extra services are available.
- Your key selling points (KSP's).
- Supporting documentation.
- Caveats.
- Costs.
- Conclusion.

Executive Summary

The executive summary – an important part of your proposal:
- The real deciders will not be reading the entire bid – they will rely on their technical reviewers – but the executive summary should sell to them in easy to understand descriptions.
- It summarizes your strengths as well as your bid
- It sets out your stall!

FastTrack© Bid Management

The Best Company – it explains why you are.
You do know why you are the best company in your field?
- What are your differentiators?
- What is the best thing that you do?
- Do not mention other companies by name!

Solution
You should include:
- Technical solution – how it will be done.
- Project management – what processes will be used.
- Staffing – who will do it.
- Support – how it will be supported and maintained.
- Other services available – a good place for your selling hooks.
- Risks and issues – explain them to your client and how you will mitigate or avoid them.
- Compliance – some bid managers use a "cleaned up" version of their Compliance Matrix in the executive summary as a selling tool.
- Cultural factors – a bid for China is totally different to one for the USA – get cultural advice if need be.

Selling Hooks
These are the points that you want your client to remember. Use your sales or marketing team to help you make them:
- Pertinent.
- Short and pithy.
- Standing out.
- Memorable!

FastTrack© Bid Management

Key Selling Points
These are your differentials:
- What can you do that is better than all other potential bidders?
- What can you do best for your client?
- How can you make your proposal memorable?

Support Documentation
These are mostly standard documentation to back up your proposal and will consist of the following:
- Product descriptions.
- Diagrams, plans and pictures.
- CV's, resumes and job descriptions
- Support and maintenance contracts.
- Company descriptions.
- Balance sheets and other published financials.

Caveats
Remember when you set up your risk matrix and Compliance Matrix? Your caveats should now come from there. They should be:
- Not too obvious but understandable
- Pertinent and polite

Costs
Work from your pricing model:
- Use the structure as set out in the ITT
- Include everything
- Make it competitive
- Define if taxes, delivery etc included

FastTrack© Bid Management

Conclusion

The last thing they read so the last thought on your bid. Should include:

- Thanks for the opportunity of bidding.
- Summarize your strengths.
- Benefits of using your company.
- Other options available to the client.
- The way forward.

VIP: Give your evaluators something to remember you by as they move onto the next bid to evaluate. If you are lucky, they will then be checking the other bid against yours to see how the others measure up.

Other Bits and Bobs

- Table of contents.
- Headers and footers.
- Confidentiality clauses.
- Covering letter.
- Glossary of terms.
- Brochures.
- Contact details.
- CD/DVD copy.

VIP: In the heat of the moment – do not forget all the little things. I know of bids that have been lost because they were non compliant by forgetting something that was compulsory.

Bid Presentation

In this section, you will learn how to present an eye catching winning bid. Hide those weaknesses and accentuate the strengths.

We just put it all together don't we?

Read the RFP now go back and read it again!

Why is the presentation of your bid so important?
- It takes you from Wish to Win.
- Presents your good points.
- Hides your weaknesses.
- Keeps the evaluator's attention.

Presentation is vital to ensure:

- **Hitting those hot spots:** By reading the RFP thoroughly and from feedback from your sales people, you should know what your potential client's particular interests or "want to have's" are. Make sure that you address these hot spots, subtly but definitely there.
- **Graphics and text**: It is true a picture does paint a thousand words. Bids can be technical and somewhat boring and are not always read by technical people. Use a graphic or picture to show part of the solution/service and then explain it underneath.

FastTrack© Bid Management

– **Easy on the eye**: As an experienced evaluator reading up to 10 bids on the same subject, I can tell you that a proposal that reads well and is comfortable to read is a blessing and always well remembered.

– **Making your point:** Clarity and succinctness in a proposal is a good indicator of the quality of the products and services that may be produced. Will you client want a project that rambles on and on and never seems to conclude?

– **Subtly offering extra services:** The key word is subtle. Indicate within your bid that you are offering what your client wants, but can offer so much more that they may require in the future. Your client may think that best company to start a relationship with is the one that they can grow with.

Preparation

Collect together:
- Standard data.
- The solution.
- Assumptions.
- Exceptions.
- Costs.
- Brochures.
- Covering letter.
- CD/DVD copies if required.
- All the odds and bobs that were also required.

Do not forget
- Your bid should reflect your company's brand.
- Use standard templates, including your sub contractor's contribution.

A short note on your cover letter: This should be used to present your proposal in its best light. It should be just under one page long, formally written and addressed to the key member of your potential client's evaluation team (found from the ITT). Do not forget to include you key selling points (subtly – this is a letter).

The Proposal Structure

Who are your audience?

- **The deciders** who will read the executive summary as well as feedback from the other evaluators.
- **The business** who will need a non-technical explanations to meet their expectations.
- **Technical reviewers** who will require deep technical information.
- **Evaluators** who will read everything as well as supporting information for those who wish to delve deeper.

QUESTION

Where is the best place to put your key selling points in the main body of the proposal?

Presentation Golden Rules

Remember:

- Follow any required presentation standards.
- Make your presentation reflect your brand and image.
- Consistency, consistency, consistency!
- Key information in the top 1/3rd of the page.
- Use lots of white so that it is easy to read.
- Use graphics to explain and inform.

Here is the best way to set out your proposal.

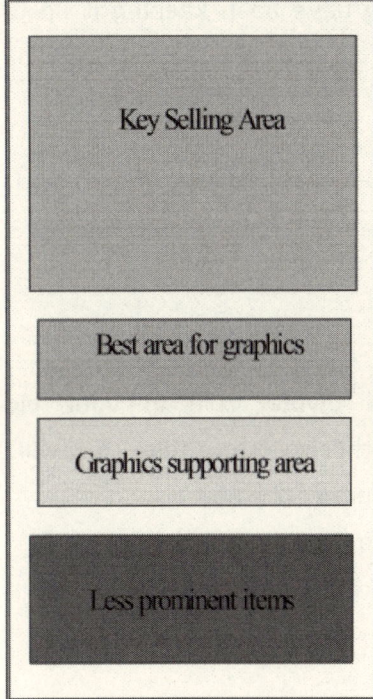

Bid Production

It is late, everyone is tired, the deadline is looming and the bid is in pieces all over the place. There must be an easier way?

Now can we just gather the stuff together?
- Yes but how do you know what your need?
- Who's got it?
- How it all fits together?

Remember you Bid Plan? - You have been keeping it up to date?

Your plan will have:
- Who's got what?
- Where it goes in the bid.

Bid Administration

Your bid administrator is the pivotal role in your bid production. Please do not forget this important role- they will:
- Ensure all content is delivered on time.
- Ensure a consistent design.
- Manage the bid library.
- Maintain the templates.
- Collate the bid content.
- Maintain version control.

In addition, generally chase around making sure the bid is produced and collected together in your War Room.

FastTrack© Bid Management

War Room

This is where the bid preparation takes place- it will be:

– Quiet and secure so that you can work without fear that your good works will get out. In very secure bids – remember to shred your papers and secure your computers.

– Fully equipped to make the bid preparation and production so much easier.

– Have wall charts and plans so that everyone knows what is where and when.

– Stocked with supplies so that you can get on with the bid production.

– Have refreshments for those long times ahead.

Assigning Work

Do not forget to let people know what their role is in this frenzied time. You should have:

– Administrators and collators.
– Red team, which is the quality team.
– Financial team who will provide the final pricing.
– Factory workers who will put the bid together.
– Legals, the final checkers to protect your company.
– Bid sponsor, who will give the final OK.

The Red Team

These are a group of people, not involved with the bid preparation. They will:
- View the bid as if they were the client.
- Undertake a final quality check.
- Undertake a risk mitigation check.
- Provide a final reasonableness check.

Subcontractors

Do not forget to manage their contribution and ensure that it is:
- On time.
- To quality.
- To their remit.
- To the agreed cost.

Costing

Your costing team should now be coming to the final bid price:
- In correct format as per the ITT. You do not have to make all your calculations common knowledge.
- In correct currency and you have set up your hedging account?
- Taxes and delivery accounted for.

The Factory

The factory is where is all put together:

– Conveyor belt format seems to be the best way. So long tables and good organization.

– Several printers helps speed up preparation.

– Multiple copiers makes duplication a lot quicker.

– Structured and controlled, your bid administrator and bid manager reign supreme here.

– Bound, so you or the evaluators do not lose vital parts of the bid.

– Signed, by your bid sponsor or someone more senior. Your bid is a contract if it wins.

I hope that you have enjoyed this book. The Bid Manager also offers consultancy to assist you in bids that are more complex.

www.Bid-Manager.com

Workshops

Workshop 1

From your chosen scenario:
- What possible risks can you identify?
- How would you mitigate them?
- What logistical problems can you identify?
- How would you manage this bid?

Workshop 2

From your chosen scenario:
- Define your bidding strategy
- Outline a potential solution and what particular activities will need to be undertaken.
- How would you control this bid?

Workshop 3

From your chosen scenario:
- Set up your pricing model
- Define a suitable bid management team
- Define an appropriate project management team
- How would you control this bid?

Workshop 4

Set-up your own company bid management environment.

1) What standard documents would you expect to have available at the start of a bid?

2) What facts would you require to decide upon an informed bid strategy?

3) What selling hooks would your company have?

4) What are your key selling points in your company's area of expertise?

5) What articles would you expect to find in your War Room?

6) What articles would you expect to find in your factory?

Scenario 1 - Croatia

You are authorized to prepare a bid for a £25m billing system for a telecoms company in Croatia, to be delivered in 1 year, funded by international loan, using mostly local labor.

Scenario 2 – New Technology

You are bidding for a major new project that involves a client with whom you wish to foster a closer working relationship. The bid is for an innovative technology that is high risk. You do not wish to upset your client but wish to make a profit on the bid. Define your bid strategy that will meet all these needs.

Scenario 3 – National Bingo

To benefit from the national boom in Bingo and put some extra money in the UK government coffers the government has decided to launch a national Bingo Game. The key details are:

- The balls will be drawn on BBC1 at 15-minute intervals, 3 balls at a time.
- All claims will be by SMS messaging to one text number and one national telephone number.
- There will be 100 numbers and each card will have 5 rows of 5 numbers. Wins are in the usual manner.
- Cards will be sold via small shops etc as per the National Lottery. All cards are random.

The bid is to design and set up:
- The call centre communications
- The text centre communications
- Comms from the live draw to the call and text centers.
- Training and support of appropriate call and text centre staff.
- Set up of technical support desk.

Scenario 4 – Manchester Olympics

Manchester is placing a bid for the next Olympic Games and requires you to produce a tender for the following:
- Timings and recordings of the track events.
- Timings and recordings of the swimming events.
- Timings and recordings of the marathon.

Scenario 5 – Contact your MP

To build upon the momentum of the eGovernment initiative it has been decided that the voter should be able to contact their MP electronically. The government proposes that each MP is available via:

- A "Contact your MP" website and email service.
- A SMS centre that will redirect SMS messages to the appropriate MP.
- An E-government Call Centre that will collate queries and give them to the appropriate MP.
- The bid is to design and set up:
- The call centre communications
- The text centre communications
- Server, email capabilities and network for the website.
- Training of appropriate web, call and text centre staff.
- Set up of technical support desk.

Scenario 6 – Reality Game Show

Channel 5 has decided that it needs its own reality show and has come up with the great concept. "Swap your Kids". Several families will be set up in a small estate of houses. During the month of daily broadcasts, the families will all "Swap their Kids." It is expected that there will be considerable problems that arise over the month – mainly because the families have been chosen to ensure this. At each problem, the viewers will be asked to vote on one of 5 options. Trained child and adult psychologists will be on hand to advise. One family every two weeks will be voted out by the viewers and several tasks will be set. The winner gets three weeks in Orlando for the Kids and three weeks around the world for the adults only.

The bid is for:
- Setting up the communications within each house on the estate to the TV centre.
- Setting up the communication loop between the presenter, the TV centre and the families.

Scenario 7 – Royal Move

An unnamed but prominent Royal wishes to set up a small, out of the way, discrete house for him and his partner. The existence of the partner is not in the public domain and must remain so. You will liaise with the Palace Senior Staff to ensure this. The bid is for:
- Managing the move.
- Setting up internal intranet for entertainment and security purposes.
- Setting up the security environment.

Scenario 8 – Major Out Sourcing

A major insurance company wishes to outsource its call centers to another country with a view to saving a considerable amount of money. This bid is for:
- Designing the new call centre.
- Evaluating bids from various companies to run the call centre.
- Managing the move to the new call centre.
- Redesigning the business processes within the company.
- Managing the layoff or retraining of the current staff.

FastTrack© Bid Management

Answers

QUESTION

How does Bid Management differ from Project Management?

ANSWER

You should mention such items as:

– Difference in the time frames, with a fixed end date.

– Heavy emphasize on risk management and presentation.

– Very legally constrained.

– Very marketing biased.

– Very horizontal management structure.

– Different tools – for example a MsProject project plan will not work!

QUESTION

What is the importance of bid reviews?

ANSWER

Your answer should include factors such as:

– The need to make frequent staged reviews so that money and time are not lost during the bid life cycle.

– The need to produce a quality, risk mitigated, correctly costed bid.

– Frequent reviews keep the bid on track and to the strategy.

FastTrack© Bid Management

QUESTION

Your hardware kit does not meet all the requirements but exceeds others. How would you manage this within your Compliance Matrix?

ANSWER

You should be looking at presenting the points that exceed the requirements as being of stronger benefit than those that do not meet. If they do not meet because the spec is wrong or out of date then be careful how you word this. Your caveat should be positive.

"We more than exceed your requirements with respect to x, whilst we do not quite meet your compliance for y then we feel that our z more than compensates and will actually give you a better xxxxx"

QUESTION

Can you think of a situation when your company will go ahead with a bid that will lose money?

FastTrack© Bid Management

ANSWER

A possible situation may be:

– When you are able to build enough teasers, upgrades etc so that you can still make money, and have bid low in order to win the bid.

– When winning the bid gives your company a significant profile in the client's company.

– When the value of support and maintenance is significant and/or allows you a "footprint" in the client company.

– When your hardware, software or services tie your client to your company.

QUESTION

What is the difference between a copyright and an IPR (intellectual property right)?

ANSWER

A copyright is made on an item or product – e.g. software, book etc. The IPR is the thought process that goes into making the product. So sell the copyright on a book about boats and you buyer is the only one who can duplicate the book for future sales. Sell the IPR and you cannot ever write about those types of boats again! The best way is to license the item. This gives the purchaser the right to use the article for an agreed time period, and you can sell the book to others.

FastTrack© Bid Management

QUESTION

Where is the best place to put your key selling points?

ANSWER

As a quick experiment count to 10, then pick up a newspaper or book where you can look at two pages at once. What part of the paper or book gets your first attention? It is the top $1/3^{rd}$ of the left hand side of the paper/book. This is because the western world reads top to bottom and left to right. It therefore makes sense to put your key selling points in this position.

Index

A

Assigning Work · 65

B

Bid Administrator · 21, 26, 31, 33
Bid Controls · 25
Bid Definition · 55
Bid factory · 29, 33
Bid Manager · 2, 11, 19, 28, 31, 67
Bid Managers · 12
Bid Plan · 20, 31, 64
Bid Presentation · 60
Bid Production · 64
Bid Reviews · 22
Bid Sponsor · 18, 19, 28
Bid Strategy · 19, 34, 38
Bid Structure · 56
Bid Tool Kit · 29

C

Caveats · 20, 29, 32, 56, 58
Compliance Matrix · 5, 19, 20, 30, 32, 57, 58, 74
Copyrights · 41, 45, 48
Cost Control · 25
Costing · 66
Costs · 51, 56, 58, 61

D

Decision Stage · 17
Design Control · 26
Design Templates · 33
Dispute Process · 48

E

Executive Summary · 56

F

Financial Risks · 42
Force Majeure · 41, 45, 48

I

Internal Risks · 43, 51

K

Key Selling Points · 19, 30, 36, 38, 58

L

Lee Lister · 2
Legal Notice · 9

N

Non Compliance · 37

P

Payment Schedule · 49
Penalties · 42, 45, 50
Preparation Stage · 19, 20
Pricing Stage · 20
Production Stage · 21
Project Risks · 42

Q

Quality Reviews · 23

R

Red Team · 28, 33, 66
RFP · 22, 23, 28, 37, 40, 41, 43, 44, 45, 55, 60

Risk · 19, 20, 22, 23, 24, 25, 28, 31, 36, 39, 40, 41, 44, 45, 50, 51, 52, 53
Risk Control · 25
Risk Reviews · 23

S

Selling Hooks · 37, 38, 57
Solution Control · 25
Stage Processes · 16
Strategy Stage · 18, 19
SuperBid Methodology · 15, 29

T

The Bid Manager". · 2
The Bid Team · 27
The Factory · 67
The Invitation to Tender · 14
The Pricing Model · 31
The Proposal Structure · 62

W

War Room · 29, 32, 65
Workshops · 68

Printed in Great Britain by
Amazon.co.uk, Ltd.,
Marston Gate.